DEAR BRITTANY

DEAR BRITTANY

GAWJJ

Rev. date: 01/08/2015

To order additional copies of this book, contact:
Xlibris
1-888-795-4274
www.Xlibris.com
Orders@Xlibris.com
551990

CONTENTS

Written with love to all my family and friends

THE NEIGHBORHOOD

Congratulations! We finally did it...completed our book of poems. Wow!

And, now, what is our next project? Shall we continue to write and to dream?

Why not?

We find great joy in the pen. We can talk to each other and to others. We must remember that we are writing for the generations to come... our generations. Do you think that the family will create an author within the next generation, as well?

These ventures are so exciting. I cannot wait to continue telling tales about the family and the neighborhood. The neighborhood in all its uniqueness was a fascinating community of hard working laborers, domestic workers, factory laborers and a few professional; as well.

Seaport Town was a small community of family and friends. All the people knew one another. Whether we lived in town or in the country, we still knew all of the folk in Seaport Town, the oyster hub of the area... population twenty thousand.

We could divide the community by its churches. There were four small churches on the side of town... where all the Black folks lived.

Most of the folks attended the Christ Pentecostal Church. The Pentecostal church boasted of shouting spirit-filled preachers. The musicians were the envy of the other churches in East Seaport. All of their musicians could play multiple instruments, sing, and write songs.

The Greater Hope A.M.E. Church and St. James A.M. E. Zion Church faced one another on opposite sides of Franklin Street which was the main thoroughfare in the heart of East Seaport. At any time of a day, Franklin Street was bustling with traffic and business.

Mr. Ned's Barbershop was on the north end of the street. Across the street from the barbershop was the Grear's Garage and gas station owned by Mr. Ned's brother, Jonathan Grear. The Harold, a two-story hotel, stood in the middle of the block.

Cousin Ned's Hot Dog and Shoe Shine stand was crunched between two apartment buildings. And, next door to the three buildings was Pop's Taxi and and candy store.

On the south end of the busy street, was Muriel's Luncheonette, Ms. Ollie's Take-Out Booth, and the Saturday Night Dance Parlor. Traveling south on Franklin Street, it was hard to miss the Bar & Grill, Fisher's Package Store, and the State Service Center & Clinic. At the corner of Franklin & Douglass streets, many of the local people shopped at Manship's Grocery and Fish Market.

THE WEDDING

Just a few blocks around the corner off Douglass, on Second Street, the members of Wesley Memorial Methodist Episcopal Church were preparing for the Womanless Wedding. Most of the men were cleaning the chandeliers, washing windows, polishing the pews, oiling the chancel rails and vacuuming the floors and carpet.

The youth were cleaning the basement and making the yards and grounds attractive. They mowed the lawn, trimmed the bushes, hedges and trees. Weeds were pulled from the flower beds and new plants added to the garden areas. The place was beginning to look grandiose... fit for a king!

In the meantime, Aunt Polly was finishing Josephleon's wedding gown and the bridesmaids dresses. The members of the bridal party were either at the barber shop or beauty parlor. Mother had just added the crimpy curls to Michaelana's puffs. Jamezina, the matron of honor, was sitting under the dryer.

The three other beauticians in East Seaport were just as busy getting the bridesmaids, the families of the bride and groom dolled-up for the wedding. The bridal party promised to look like a picture from an Ebony Fashion Show?

"Josey," Mother questioned. "Are you ready for the big day?" She was talking to Josephleon who was the bride for the Womanless Wedding.

"Girl, I went downtown to the Boutique and got the prettiest lingerie," Josey cheerfully volunteered. "When you finish with me, I'll show it to you. It is in my shopping bag."

"Is Roonie excited about marrying his real sweetheart?" Mother quizzed Josey.

"He better be or else, he'll wish he had shown some kind of emotions," said Josey, not able to contain her excitement!

"Did you finish that cake, Muriel?" Josey asked.

"It is the prettiest cake that I have ever made, I do believe," Mother chirped proudly. "After I finish your hair, I'll show you. It's a beauty!"

"I can't wait to see it and to taste it," Josey said, licking her lips and rolling her eyes.

"Where is the honeymoon?" Mother inquired– as an after-thought.

"That's his call. I am just waiting to see where that fool plans to take us and it better be farther than Harold's Hotel!" Josey exclaimed.

The laughter and giggles filled the parlor. Everyone knew that Josey was serious and expected something outstanding from Roonie.

Miss Telma and Miss Gladys had finished decorating the church and the basement for the reception. With the fresh flowers from her garden, Miss Telma adorned the sanctuary and the basement with huge baskets of colorful roses, lilacs, and gladiolus. Rainbow-colored crepe paper draped the sanctuary pews and the basement tables. Bouquets of colorful flowers filled the windows. It was beginning to look like a wedding.

The Womanless Wedding was an annual fund-raiser for the Trustees Board and the Building Fund Committee. It had become their dream to build a Fellowship Hall on the property adjacent to the church. Youth programs and outreach ministries were to be housed in the new fellowship hall.

The Womanless Wedding was sold-out. As the party began, the cameras flashed. Folks stretched their necks to see everything and everyone. You could hear the crowd as they whispered, "Oh, look at that beautiful gown! The bridal party dresses were exquisite … a picture out of a fashion magazine. No two dresses were the same style or color. Everything was in the colors of the rainbow.

The groom wore white. The groomsmen wore rainbow colored suits to match the colors of the bridesmaids dresses. The bridal party included six bridesmaids and six groomsmen, a best man, a matron of honor, a ring-bearer, a flower girl, and a preacher; not to forget the videographer, photographer, organist and soloist… all were men.

The groom was about five feet tall in his stocking feet. The bride stood five feet-eleven in her spiked heels. Folks in the audience had to stand up to see the groom amidst the rest of the wedding party.

As a signal that the wedding ceremony had ended, the church bells rang softly. As soon as the reception ended, the bridal party moved slowly up the steps ready to go home, leave the church and end the long active day. Suddenly, the crowd was pushing its way up the stairs. There was a clamor of noise and much confusion. The crowd was out of control.

"Just stand back and give her some air," Rooney said – pushing the crowd out of the area. "Get back, please!"

The bridesmaids knelt to comfort and caress Josey who was unconscious and unaware of all the attention that he was getting. The crowd waited anxiously for someone to let them know what to expect and anticipate.

Everyone was talking at the same time, "What's wrong? What is the problem? Who is hurt? Is it Rooney or Josey? What happened?"

Josey was air-lifted to New County Hospital to consult with a specialist... a cardiologist. What an uncanny culmination for such a beautiful occasion.

MISS OLGA

We could always look out the back door and see Miss Olga's house. She and all the ladies in the neighborhood enjoyed their task of watching and observing what all of us were doing. They never seemed to miss much – if anything.

It was their fun activity, we thought, to spy on us and then rat on us. We started to play a game of hide and seek. We thought we were hiding from their eyes, but as we soon learned and began to say, "The Shadow knows the books of senior." Now don't ask me what that meant or where we found it or how we started it, but it was from one of those spy movies; so we decided to coin the phrase.

We called all the ladies in town Miss Myra, Miss Agnes, Miss Mayjune, Miss "Somebodies First Name." Miss Olga insisted, however, on some occasions on letting us know who she was.

"It's Olga Mayolonna Stanley Fitchett Sloen Benson." She would say with a slight lisp.

"She just enjoys telling her name and letting everyone know that she has outlived three husbands." The word moved around the porch. The women were having their fun now, bringing up things they could share. They shared the same old stories all the time. I knew them by heart.

Sometimes Aunt Etta would tell the story. Other times Aunt Anna would change the story. More often than not, Aunt Edith would add more to it than was true. And then, all of the sisters would laugh.

"Well, I heard, that she's got a new man over there. He'll be the next one to either marry her or to die or both – if he's not careful." Someone lied. And, they all screamed with laughter.

It was a Sunday afternoon and my grandmother's sisters and families came by for dinner and a visit. They came after church and stayed until dusk.

"Well, who is this one?' a sister asked.

"He's an older man. Close to her own age, whatever that is," Etta added.

"He works at the oyster house. That's where she found him, I heard," Anna chuckled. "Dutch said he's good at shucking oysters, though. Real good!"

Just then a little short, dark, handsome, elderly gentleman walked through the back yard. He turned, smiled at the ladies, tipped his hat and said, "Good afternoon, Ladies."

Together the sister chorused, "Good afternoon!" They could not say his name, for they did not know it. The man moved quickly and deliberately into Miss Olga's house.

As soon as he closed the door, the porch was filled with such hooting and hollering and screaming of laughter that Mom Minnie came on the porch to see what all the fuss was about… to which she added, "He's a good church-going man, too. He was in church this morning. He said that he was going to join the choir. Beat that?!"

"She can sure enough catch em, now. She don't waste no time. Gets one in the grave and finds another at the grave yard. She's a fast worker."

Wednesday night, Miss Olga and Mr. Gowens came to choir practice. Everyone watched as Mr. Gowens removed his hat, took Miss Olga's arm and helped her up in the choir box – and then graciously bowed.

"Now I just can't believe any man is that good," Sister Marie bellowed. "He ain't real. Aint't no man that good."

But everything seemed to make Mr. Gowens that good. He was a peaceful, calm, quiet-spoken gentleman. And, Miss Olga had found him.

The choir was practicing old hymns for Sunday service. "We'll sing Hymn number two twenty-six. We can go over it briefly. All of us know that song. Let's sing, please," that was the voice of the choir director, Aunt Polly.

Aunt Polly was the choir director and musician. She was the only musician at Wesley. Wesley did not have a drum or guitar or tambourines. Most of the family sang in the choir. Muriel and Mom Minnie sang in the alto section. The rest of the family sang whatever note they could carry, "So low you can't hear them," was Uncle Alonza's so called funny remark.

The choir sang out melodiously. Miss Olga sang louder than usual. Sister Marie whispered, "Trying to impress the man…" And the choir members snickered in agreement.

As usual, Miss Olga was dressed in layers of clothing. The black cotton short-sleeve blouse covered a green t-shirt a souvenir of Coney Island. A pink long-sleeved sheer blouse hidden beneath the blouses was tucked snuggly inside a pair of khaki pants covered by a grey denim skirt. Accenting the layer of blouses, she wore a blue cross-stitched sweater that was turned wrong- side-out. If one were to glance down at her feet, they could see thick brown cotton stockings under a pair of white lace-trimmed socks inside one brown and one black oxford. No one ever thought Miss Olga would grab the Best Dressed title; needless to say …the best man.

With the hymnal upside down, Miss Olga sang lustily, "Nero my dog has fleas. Nero to thee. Nero my dog has fleas. Nero to thee."

THOUGHT: "Laughter is the shout of a joyful heart."

MISS MARIE

Let me describe the neighborhood. From our backyard one could see that side of the town; for there were several other parts of East Seaport. The neighborhood formed a square. Second Street, on the west, was bordered by Hill Street on north and around the corner of Hill to the east was Street Road and Douglass Street to the south. The full area was about one-quarter of a mile in diameter circumference.

We could look at the clothes lines, water pumps, toilets, pig-pens, chicken coops, gardens, fences, junk cars, woodsheds, trees, bushes, grape vines, and flag poles. We could see the children playing softball, shooting marbles, jumping rope, playing hop scotch or patty cake.

The back yards were places for living, visiting, socializing, and signifying. It was the social center of the neighborhood.

"What's that Miss Pudding got hanging on her clothes line? I ain't never seen that before." The sisters were sharing again.

"Mother, can I go over to Miss Marie's and play with Peggy for a while. I won't stay long, please?"

"Okay, Geryl. You tell Miss Marie that I said it was okay for you to come over there." Muriel continued to share with her aunts and the other ladies; as they looked around the neighborhood from their own back porch.

Peggy met Geryl at the door. "My mom wants us to help her with the numbers, tonight, Geryl. So hurry and come in before the broadcast begins. We can't miss any numbers, you know!"

Geryl moved quickly. Inside the house It was hard to find a place to sit. Everything was in piles on top of everything. To find the radio, Peggy moved the basket filled with clean clothes that Miss Marie was to starch and iron for the Newton family downtown on the west side of Seaport Town.

The radio was blasting loudly. "Turn the radio down some, Peggy," Miss Marie ordered.

The two girls listened intently to the broadcast. The horse races at Triple Downs were broadcast over the radio, daily. Geryl and Peggy were to write the race results down and total t how the horses placed in the first three races.

"Coming in near the home stretch, running strong around the track is Blessed Beauty number fifteen. The horses are running neck and neck. As they come to the home stretch Miss Lucky Leaf number nine is in first place. Running a few paces behind Lucky Leaf is My Time # 6. It's a photo finish! No! The winner is My Time #4. Finishing second was Miss Lucky Leaf number nine and dragging behind in third place was Prince George # 11; beating Blessed Beauty by a nose." The announcer had finished the results of race number three.

Peggy and Geryl were to write down the three winners for the first, second, and third races. The total numbers divided by three would give you the number for each of the three races. The three numbers for the day were 658 - the number for the day.

Miss Marie would tell the number runners the results of the races and the number for the day. The number runner would have to pay off any winner on their circuit. On the East side of Seaport Town, the regular number player would pay fifty cents or a nickel or a dime and write down their chosen number. If they hit or won, they were paid by the number runner.

In the Valley, the name that everyone used to define the neighborhood square, Mr. Baker had won five dollars. He had played 658 for fifty-cents; therefore, he won ten times fifty cents or five dollars. Had he played that number for one dollar, he would have won ten dollars. The runner received a dollar of the winnings under twenty dollars.

"If the number played was boxed, Mr. Baker would have won ten dollars. Mr. Baker could have played 568 and the number came out, as it did, 658, he would have won ten dollars. To box a number, you pay a minimum of one dollar." Geryl explained to Muriel who "flipped-her-lid" when she found out what they had done at Miss Marie's house.

"You are not allowed to go there again, do you hear me, Missy?" Muriel was practically stammering.

STEPPING FREELY

Stepping Freely was the name given to James Freeman. He was an outstanding dancer. He ran like a champion and galloped like a stallion around the track. On the dance floor he was a Sammy Davis, Jr.; winning most of the contests on Saturday nights at the Saturday Night Dance Hall on Franklin Street.

Stepping and Muriel were the dance champions of East Seaport. They had won dance contest in Maryland and Virginia. Muriel put their trophies on a shelf behind the counter in the restaurant. They were proud of their accomplishments. Both Stepping and Muriel loved to dance.

His one major fault was that Stepping could not manage to stay out of jail. Stepping Freely lived on Second Street off the Valley with his mother, aunt, and two brothers. They were faithful members at Christ Pentecostal Church. Both his mother and aunt were Sunday school teachers and worked in the community cleaning for the President of City Bank and the Mayor of Seaport Town.

Steppin Freely was forever getting into some type of mischief or trouble. He was often in the wrong place at the wrong time or found doing the wrong things at the wrong times. The last time Stepping Freely was jailed, he was charged for writing bad checks. In jail, he attended church services, led worship, sang in the choir, and repented of his sins.

Steppin Freely joined Christ Pentecostal Church again for the fourth or fifth time. He vowed to walk the straight and narrow pathway and be obedient to the Word of God.

"I'm born again!" he told his mother. "You'll see!"

Stepping Freely worked hard at the Old Chicken Plant down on the River Front. He attended church regularly, paid his tithes, studied the Bible, and found time to help with the Men's Fellowship.

One Saturday afternoon, Stepppin Freely went from house to house in the Valley selling chickens to practically everyone in the neighborhood. He did well. All the chickens were sold.

Just before dusk, the county sheriff issued warrants for all the neighbors in the Valley. Down town at Court # 7, the charge was that of receiving stolen goods. They could have received a more severe charge of aiding and abetting. Nonetheless, not a person was spared from the charge or the fine. Stepping Freely returned to jail.

The next day, in our church Wesley Memorial, Rev. James' sermon was Exodus 20:15, "Thou shalt not steal!" Ironically as it may seem, that same message was probably being preached in each of the churches on the east side of Seaport Town. Most of the neighbors were trying to forget the chicken deal they had made with Stepping Freely. They were ashamed!

It was testimony time and, as usual, Mr. Christopher was running around the church screaming and yelling, calling on the name of Jesus. His regular routine was to shout, "And the Lord shook me and He shook me. And, he shook the devil right out of me."

Today Brother Chris' testimony was just a little different. He jumped out of his shoes and shouted, "And the Lord shook me, and shook me, and He shook the shit right out of me."

Miss Marie shouted, "Amen!" She turned and whispered to Sister Telma, "Now, that's the closest thing to the truth that I have ever heard him say!"

Mom Minnie's brother Alonza would tell her, "Minnie your people, only you colored people, worry God to death; asking for this and begging for that. You get on His last nerves."

Mom Minnie softly responded, "You know, Alonza, the church is a hospital for sinners. That's what I have been told and have heard."

Alonza retorted, "You mean an asylum for the demented and touched in the head."

Aunt Edith smirked, "Alonza, in that case, you should make your bed in the church and not in hell like you're doing."

THE TRUNK

The children were playing in the lot near Second Street. They were playing stick ball. Some were fighting and others were just standing around – doing nothing.

"Don't let that ball go in Miss Casey's yard. She will keep it. Please throw the ball in the other direct- ......" Peggy was yelling to her team mates, but too late.

The ball had gone through the gate into Ms. Casey's yard. "I'm not going in there to get it. You go!" Peggy told Geryl.

"Not me," Geryl whispered scared to go anywhere near Ms. Casey house; knowing that she would also get a tongue lashing from her mother.

"Send Emory, let him go," Peggy told Geryl.

The girls picked Emory to go in the yard to get the ball. Emory lived off Franklin Street near St. James A.M.E. Zion Church. He didn't get down on Second Street too often. And, besides, he was the youngest one in the bunch.

Geryl and Peggy were playing with most of the kids who lived on the Douglass Street side of the Valley. The Waldins lived on that side of the Valley. Ben Waldin was Muriel's brother. Ben's children and grandchildren were gathered in the lot to play with Geryl, Peggy, Emory and the other five or six children who had gone to the lot to "kid around."

Emory came back to the lot with the ball in hand, running fast and out of breathe. The children were laughing; for they thought that Ms. Casey had run him out of her yard.

"She got you didn't she?" the laughter was dense.

21

"No, I didn't see anyone. I just heard screams and yelling." Emory was nervously shaking.

"Boy, you are serious." Peggy slapped him on the back.

"I heard someone in the house yelling for help." Emory stuttered and stammered.

"What did they say?" asked Yvonne, one of Ben's grandchildren.

"Let me out of here! Help!" Emory was talking fast and shaking.

The children moved closer to the house. They crept through the back gate and into the yard. Peggy motioned for everyone to remain quiet and not to make a sound; for two reasons. First of all, they did not want Ms. Casey to hear them; and, finally, they wanted to hear what Emory thought he had heard.

The children practically ran over each other as they pushed to get out of the yard.

They heard a voice yelling, "Help, let me out of here." The banging sounds were louder than the screaming and yelling.

"When we arrived at Uncle Ben's house, Aunt Myrtle told us to calm down and speak clearly; so that she could understand what we were saying. She said that she could not hear us all talking at the same time." Geryl was telling the story to her great aunts who were still sitting on the back porch – sharing natter.

"I am not going near Ms. Casey's house ever again. It's too spooky!" Geryl breathed a sigh of relief… just to be home and close to family - again.

"You know that crazy Edward. On the Saturdays that he goes to work, he locks Beulah in a trunk in his room. He bolts the trunk with a lock and takes the key to work with him. Even his mother, Ms. Casey, doesn't have a key." Ethel was sharing the story with the sisters.

"He says that while he is at work, she might try to run away with another man," Anna spoke her thoughts, "What a blessing that would be for Beulah. That would be a blessing for Beulah."

"Bless her heart!" said Mom Minnie. "Bless her heart!"

BULLYING

Matthew invented bullying in Seaport Town. He teased people, pulled hair, tripped anyone, and punched whoever disagreed with him. And, that was on a good day. If he were having a bad day, it's hard to know what he just might do.

Matthew Coleman was in the sixth grade for the third time. He was nearly sixteen years old – just waiting for the day that he could quit school. In the meantime, he played hookey, was late or truant from school. Miss Lynn the Truant Officer frequented his house.

He wanted to quit school, but his mother and grandfather would not let him. So, whenever he came to school, he created havoc! Once there was a terrible accident as the buses were leaving the grounds. Everyone believes that Matthew pushed Victor in the path of the bus.

As the driver was moving the bus backward to wiggle out of a tight space, he did not see Victor who had run in back of the bus. Victor suffered severe brain injury and damage from which he was diagnosed as never to recover. No one saw what happened before the bus hit Victor. But, if you lead a violent life; you become a suspect.

Matthew sat in the sixth grade class throwing spit balls and kicking anyone who came near his desk. He pulled up Peggy's skirt, slapped Emory behind the head, cussed at Yvonne, and pulled the elastic in the waistline of my skirt. Today was dress-up day. We were celebrating Black History Month with a contest and assembly. The students were to select a famous African American, dress the part and participate in the Black History Program as that person.

I was Harriet Tubman. I had worn a floor-length black skirt and a long-sleeve white blouse with a ruffled front. My head was wrapped in a grey scarf - topped with a wide-brimmed yellow straw hat.

After Matthew tried to pull my skirt down, that was it. With little or no thought, I left my seat, jumped on his chest, knocked him in the floor and put my knee in his collar. He was choking. Immediately, I pulled both sides of his tie until he could hardly breathe. He was gasping for breath. No one came to his rescue… or to mine for that matter. Ms. Mitchell sat at her desk observing everything without saying a word.

Matthew jumped up from the floor with his tie in hand and fussing. He turned to Ms. Mitchell and yelled, "You didn't do anything! You didn't say anything to her. Did you see what she did to me? Aren't you going to do something to her?"

"Did you bother her, Mr. Coleman?" Ms. Mitchell was actually smiling. "Have a seat, sir. Thank you!"

That afternoon I stayed after school to help Ms. Mitchell grade papers. "Teacher's Pet!" the class chanted.

As I neared the front door, Faye Jean and Fran met me crying and panting. "That boy from Philadelphia, he shot at us with a bow and arrow," they cried.

"He's mean!" Faye Jean was crying and Fran was whining.

I was thinking, "How many bullies can you face in one day!?"

Frank Baker was standing in the back yard, looking mean, and threatening…just waiting for me – I guess.

"Okay. You can leave the yard, sir, please." I requested.

He stood there. "Did you shoot at my sisters with a bow and arrow?" was my silly question.

He laughed. "And I'll do it again. I'll shoot you!" he threatened.

By this time I am in his face and confronting him. I grabbed the bow and arrow, cracked it across my knee and threw it in his direction.

"Are you crazy, girl?" he remarked, looking puzzled.

"Yes!" was my short answer.

After much time for silence, "Now leave our yard and don't come back again," were my orders to him.

"I'll get you. You little -"

"The names he called me, Mother. I was tired after one day of mess and mess and mess."

I chased that bully home to his Uncle Milton with an axe that I grabbed from the wood pile. He ran screaming, "Uncle Milton!"

The axe was raised high in the air and directly over his head. I felt a strong hand on my arm. My Uncle Ben had grabbed the axe – just in the nick of time.

"Praise be to God!" Mother thanked her brother and I thanked God. "Forgive me," I prayed. "I was a bully, too, Lord and I am so sorry!"

Fran and Faye Jean were still crying. They cuddled closed to me and held me near to their hearts. "Geryl," Faye Jean whispered. "He left his bike in the backyard."

"We can give the bike to Mr. Baker." I told her. "We'll take him his bike tomorrow."

The next day we pushed the bike through the Valley to Hill Street at the Baker's place.

Mr. Baker answered the door. He was cordial and friendly.

"Mr. Baker, I am sorry about yesterday," I apologized, quickly. "Here is Frankie's bike. He left it in our yard, yesterday. Can we give it to him, please?"

"Frankie went back to Philadelphia, this morning. He said that it was too rough down here for him. He wanted to go home to his mother." Mr. Barker informed us.

"We are so sorry, Mr. Baker. Maybe he will come down here again next summer?" We inquired, with our fingers crossed behind our backs.

"I don't know, Geryl," Mr. Baker was stumbling for words. "He said that your three big huge brothers helped you beat him up. He was afraid that they would come after him, again!"

Faye Jean, Fran and I looked at each other, puzzled. As we walked through the Valley and toward home, Fran asked, "What brothers? We don't have any brothers. What did he mean?"

We were glad to get home again to forget all about this different day. We held hands and skipped home together.

XXXXXXXX

Bicycle ridin nigger
Education he ain't got.
Reputation
He gots for —
Stealin, cussin,
Finger snappin
Needle drappin,
Hub cappin
Back slappin
Gum crackin.

Das dat fools car, man.
Dats his gal-durned Cadillac.
Him's ridin in style.
Das do only trans —
Poor — ta- tion
Dis heel ignoramus gots!

"Yah, well it beats walking, man!"
"Yah? It do if'n you aint gots no shoes!"

You' sick, man?
You rides dat bike to work eber day.
Works hard you do,
Fer little pay.
And hands it over to date der man
In dat jive tie, and pink-zute suit
And yellow Cadillac.
And when it rain or snowed...
He pat you on da-dd-back.

If'n ya ask him for a ride,
Cause yo bike ain't got no heater, do it?
No stereo tape deck, no air . . .
Uh . . . conditioner, no plush fur covered, push button chair,
No wind shiled wipers, mag wheels. Don't need it dat — don't
Burn no gas.
You gots ten shift der ain't ya?
Dats were its at. Shiftin dem gears.
Complicated task.
Dat pimpin of a man dats you donates your pay check to
Don't hit a lick or tap.
He's supervisor at "Stand-a-Leans,"
Sleeps til you get off da job.
Eats steak, (fela minnon) crap sue ets,
Meals likes dat
Ain't good fer ya no how.
Makes you constipated . . .
And full.
But he can jives,
Make you believe dat bike you gots
Gooder than what he rides.

And it are.
Dats a perty bike:
Mud flaps, fox tail, mirrors on both sides,
Saddle bags, numbered tag, too! And all of dat.
Sun visor, horns and bells . . .
Where you steal all dat stuff at?

"Man, I don't wanna hear dat jive!
You ain't gots noffin! And sides . . .
It beat walkin."

"Yah! It do..
If'n you ain't go no shoes."

Dear Brittany,

Neighborhoods have changed through the years. Many times, you can't find close friends and neighbors in the community. In Seaport, we enjoyed the closeness of our small town community. We knew everyone, shared their joys, sorrows, pains, happiness, and fun. Today, most neighbors do not know each other.

Try to remember that, "Jesus said unto him, 'Thou shalt love the Lord thy God with all thy heart, and with all thy soul, and with all thy mind. This is the first and great commandment. And the second is like unto it. Thou shalt love thy neighbor as thyself.'"

Love,

Gram

DADDY STUBB

Geryl was out of breath. She ran down the hill, through the field … taking the short-cut to school. When Geryl fell through the door, Mrs. Wilson was writing on the black board. No one else was in the class room. She frightened Ms. Wilson as she screamed, "Ms. Wilson!"

Ms. Wilsons' heart raced and paced. She couldn't image what had upset Geryl for her to be so excited. She prided her star pupil with common sense, good manners, and good sense. She very seldom, if ever, was in pranks with all the other children. More often than not, she always completed her homework assignments on time. She was an excellent student and nice young lady.

"What is the matter, child?"

"Listen, my name is now Gerylinda Stewart. My mother and father got married. They got married! My Daddy Stubb came home from the service. The war is over you know? And he came home! He doesn't have to fight anymore. He is now home with us for all the time." She was not taking a breath between sentences. Finally, she sat down to breathe and to grin.

"Well, Geryl, that is so nice. I am so happy for you. I'll change your name on my register, right now. Congratulations!"

"Thank you, Ms. Wilson."

When the other children came into the classroom, they wanted to know why Geryl had come to school so early. "Why didn't you wait for us?" They asked her.

She told all of the first graders her great news! Some understood and some of them didn't care one way or the other. They all soon settled down for the school day.

"Good Morning, class!"

"And they began to sing: "Good Morning! Good Morning! Good Morning to you! Good Morning! Good Morning! Oh, how do you do?"

THOUGHT: SOME DAYS DREAMS DO COME TRUE!

DREAMING

I don't remember how long I had slept. I was restless. For the third time, I woke up and had a time going back to sleep.

This time I was awakened by loud voices. Someone in the house was arguing. As I listened more intently, I recognized the voices of Daddy Stubb and Mother. I could not hear the words; but I could understand the angry voices and tones.

"Are you trying to tell me what to do?" I heard Mother speak as I moved closer to their room.

The gist of the argument had no meaning for me. I was not a part of the conflict, therefore, I failed to know the reason for the confusion.

Suddenly, I heard mother scream and tell my father, "Don't you hit me again!"

"I'll whip your big funky ass, you slut!" was his following statement.

I heard the blows and hits. "What can I do? I can't just sit here and do nothing," I thought.

I jumped on the bed and began hitting my father with a wooden leg that had fallen off of our toy table and chair set. The leg was heavy. I must have hit him several times; for he turned to hit me back. I continued to swing the table leg at him. He was angry. Mother was still screaming, "Don't you touch her!"

I tripped over the debris in the floor; dropped my defense - the table leg. He came toward me. Without my weapon, I was no good against my attacker. I ran out the door and into the dark of the night. I was embarrassed - running in my under pants and shirt. But I ran hard and fast. I turned to see him still chasing me.

For what seemed like hours, I hid in the back of the house near the trees. Thinking that things were settled and clear, I returned home. The peace and quiet were frightening.

How Shall I Forget?

Dear Brittany,

Life is incomplete and uncertain. If we live to be one-hundred and eighteen (as I so often proclaim) we will still not finish all that we hope to accomplish or attain our hopes and dreams. The only true hope that we have is in Christ Jesus. He is the Master and Finisher of our fate and our faith.

My father, Daddy Stubb, did not live with us too long. Soon he and my mother could not face their new lives together. He went back home to live with his sister, Aunt Luvenia. That dream soon turned into many nightmares.

We continued to respect and uplift our father until he died, many years later; after suffering a heart attack following an automobile accident. The Good Book tells us to, "Honor thy father and thy mother that thy days may be long upon the land which the Lord Thy God giveth thee (Exodus 20:12)."

Don't you forget! If you would remember to do just that, I'd appreciate it. Thank you.

Love,

Gram

XXXXXXXX

Once — he gave me fifty cents,
In an inebriated splurge.
Boasted of supporting me.
Once — he cried o'er a twenty he'd
given the three of us for Christmas.
Which left him nothing to
contribute to his state.
Shall I hate?
Once — he borrowed a dollar of my
Two I'd earned baby-sitting.
Once — he was a man:
He refused to let my sister date.
She was eight.
Shall I hate?

Once — she cried
As he fell in with everything he had:
Nothing.
The last, that morning
We ate.
Shall I hate?

Once — there was a happy moment
I can barely remember,
There must have been.
Once — he was my father.
Is it too late?
Shall I hate?

XXXXX

The Black man
Cradled
Neath the flowing skirt.
Cradled, cradled, cradled.
Fear!

The Black man
Pissed
Crossed the leaky floor.
Pissed, pissed, pissed.
Missed!

The Black man
Stumbled
Down the stairs.
Down, down, down.
Where?

The Black man
Mumbled
Behind the kitchen door.
Behind, behind, behind.
There.

Man?
You done been
Stumbled down, mumbled behind,
Cradled neath, pissed across.
More? More? More?

Mayonnaise and Sugar Sandwiches

"Geryl, Franny, and Faye, time to come in!" Mother yelled. It was a hot smoldering day. The sun was at its hottest and highest…noon.

"Children! I think they would stay outside all day long no matter how hot or cold it is out there." Muriel was talking to her customers. It was too hot in the restaurant to eat. The little ceiling fans were blowing hot air. The windows were wet with sweat and heat evaporation.

"It's a devils day!" laughed Henry as he slipped through the front door from across the street at the pool hall. "All dem folks in hell is trying to find some ice water."

"Well I think we've all died and gone to hell, hot as it is here!" Muriel complained. "Where in the world are those three girls? I'm…."

Her thoughts were interrupted by a burst of noise through the back door. "Mother!" the three girls screamed. They grabbed Muriel by her legs and pulled her skirt tail; forcing her to stumble into the lunch counter.

"Mother! Please! You've got to come outside! Please, Mother! Please, Mother!" Franny was yanking her arm; as she pulled her hand. "Please, Mother! Hurry!"

Geryl had not left the back door. She stood there waiting for her mother and sister to leave the restaurant and come outside. She held the back door open.

"Muriel, that Geryl ain't doing nothing but letting a bunch of flies come in this yer place – it seems to me," one of the customers chanted. Henry nodded in agreement.

"Mother, we want to show you something, please!" Geryl exclaimed. She turned to look outside and ran back out into the yard.

Faye began to cry, "Mother, you must come see this, please!"

The four of them gathered around the Model-T Ford. Muriel rushed to open the back door of the car. Her scream was heard inside the restaurant.

In no time at all, the restaurant was quiet, calm and back to normal. Muriels's eye was puffy, red and swollen shut. The girls had apologized, cried, and nursed their mother's eye, held her hand, and retired for the afternoon.

They sat in the storage room behind the kitchen where Muriel had set up a place for the children to play and rest - while she worked at the restaurant. They sat in the quiet, cool corner of the room on a blanket on the floor near the radio; and listened to Stella Dallas and the Guiding Light.

"What do you want for lunch, Faye and Fran?" Geryl asked.

Fayed pulled Geryl's hair and head close to her ear and whispered, "Can we have a mayonnaise and sugar sandwich, please, Geryl, please?"

"Why didn't Mother see what we saw? Fran asked. "Didn't you see it Faye?"

Faye shook her head as she munched and savored her mayonnaise and sugar sandwich. And in between munches and crunches muttered, Uh, Uh!"

"I can't imagine why Mother didn't see her. Can you, Geryl?" Fran asked again.

Faye whispered, "Mother said it was a bee. A bee stung her eye. Did you see the bee, Geryl?"

Geryl was convinced of what they had seen and witnessed. She smiled, sat back, relaxed and remembered – as her sisters fell off to sleep and to dream.

Geryl thought, "I saw an Angel. It was a beautiful angel dressed in a pink gown, with wings and a halo. She was so beautiful, perched on that little toad stool… just standing there. What a beautiful witness."

Theme: It will come to visions and revelations of the Lord.

WHAT SHOULD I REMEMBER?"

Dear Brittany,

That scripture tells us that the glory is not for us. We are not to boast. We are to give God the glory for all things under the sun. Witness about God and tell the truth. When you are weak, then you are made strong through Christ Jesus.

God gives us visions and the ability to discern and to know others who are just like Jesus. You will be able to know of and discern things through the grace and love of God… in sweet communion with the Almighty. The Omnipotent One will make you humble and keep you in perfect peace … if your mind is stayed on Thee. With the infilling of the Holy Spirit, you will not find jealousy, envy, hatred, gossip, back-biting, strife, deceit, or malice in your heart; for your faith, hope and trust are in Christ Jesus Our Lord. Just learn how to lean and depend on Jesus!

Love,

Gram

A Gift Of Love

Faint, the thought of breath — if not with you,

Or a prayer without a plea for you.

Nor whispered thoughts of love in bedlam sweet,

Unless that moaning was with you my sweet.

Ah! Should I cry out in the toil of sweat and strain,

The echo of that cry of life will ease the pain.

For 'twas with you I shared this grace,

And nothing else will ever take your place.

THE ELECTRIC COMPANY

Mother and Faye moved to Connecticut. Fran and I were beyond being upset. What were we to do without Faye and what was Faye to do without us? We cried for about three days. Faye was the baby girl. We did everything for her. We combed her hair, gave her a bath, washed her clothes, prepared her meals. What would happen to Faye? We just could not imagine.

We had traveled to New Haven to visit with Gran Pop Will. We did not like the place! The young folk our age moved to fast - for us. Their lives were too different. We were just slow, sheltered country girls who did not appreciate city life and culture. Yuk!!

When we visited Gran Pop, we would take the train from Wilmington to Philadelphia and on to New York City where we transferred to Grand Central Station … by cab.

On this particular day, we hailed a Yellow Cab and headed for the station. The driver talked continually: "Where you from?" he signified.

And, neither of us girls answered. We never said a word.

"Where you going," was his next question?

"Grand Central Station," was my response. I could depend on Faye and Fran not to say anything. I was the spokesperson for the trio.

Finally we arrived at our New York destination. Were we glad! We had little or no money so we only gave the driver twenty-five cents. That was all we had to spare. We could not very well give him all the money we had. We were not that foolish. I thought that for three little girls who were only fourteen, twelve and five – that was a good tip.

The driver thought differently. He was upset! He cussed us out! He called us every name you could imagine – names in the book and names not found in the book. We bravely gathered all our many bags and strolled briskly to the station... electing to ignore the remarks, the name calling; as well as the driver.

If that were not enough, just as soon as we entered the station, along comes a bum who took our bags, evidently recognizing us as innocent gullible victims. He followed us to our train and then requested money. When we refused to give him anything, he would not release our bags. I immediately called the police officer who was standing on the platform near the train.

The policeman took our bags from the bum and handed them to me. He ordered the gentleman out of our presence saying, "They did not ask you to carry their bags. You volunteered. Move along and leave them alone."

We replied, "Thank you!" to both of the gentlemen.

By the next day, we were exhausted. We had worn Mother to a thin thread by re-telling the stories of our trip, over and over and over again. We all laughed with sighs of relief. What a blessing to have survived New York City!

"Mother, the electric is off!" Geryl yelled into the telephone. "What can we do?"

"You take bus # 7 to Eastville. Then walk three blocks to the Meakings. I'll get the money from her for today's work. When you get back into the city, you take the money directly to the company. I'll call them. They will turn it back on right away.

"Okay, I'll be right there!" Geryl was nervous. She didn't want to be late getting to the bus or to the electric company. She wanted everything to go just right. She had given Fran and Faye all the instructions. "Don't leave this house until I get back. And, I especially mean you Faye Jean. Don't go anywhere. Do you hear what I've said?"

Everything was set to go. She sat waiting for the bus to take her back into the city. It was now 3 o'clock. "The place closes at 4:30. Oh, dear!" she thought. "Hurry up bus!"

She paced in front of the bus stop. No one was there. She waited impatiently and alone.

She fretted in silence. She twisted her hands and squirmed on the bench.

"It is now three-thirty. Why is the bus so late?" she thought.

"You want a ride into town?" a voice interrupted her thoughts.

She looked up and there was a car and a driver in front of her. She said, "Are you going into the city, sir?"

"Yes, Mam! I'll take you right there. Hop in!" the voice responded.

Geryl jumped enthusiastically into the huge, clean smelling car and looked directly into the face of a beady-eyed, red faced gentleman. He was smiling with a wide mouth that showed a few gold-capped teeth. His olive complexion was filled with pox and holes. His huge nose was warted on the end. He talked incessantly… on and on about nothing.

Geryl was not listening, she was thinking and discerning. His hands moved across the front seat toward Geryl.

"Where are you going little lady?" he smiled. And Geryl told him.

"I need to get there right away. Thanks, sir, for stopping to get me. I'll get there on time now. Thanks…"

Her voice trailed off as she began to notice that he had changed directions and was going away from the city.

"Where are you going!" she screamed.

"Now, little girly, I know you knew what to expect by getting in my car." He grinned and moved closer to the middle of the front seat.

"You turn this car around and take me… no let me out…now!" she calmly remarked.

And with that statement, she opened the door to the moving vehicle. "Let me out or I'll jump out of this car right here and now. LET ME OUT OF THIS CAR! NOW!"

The car slowed down to a pace speed as the door on the passenger's side of the car remained ajar. Cars in front and behind of the vehicle began to slow down and to observe them.

"Let me out of this car, right now. Do you hear me!" she whispered as she held the car door opened.

The driver pulled the car close near the next bus stop and pleaded with her to get out of his car. Geryl was livid. She sat on the bench near the bus stop and waited patiently.

"I'll just wait. We can sit in the dark. I'll get there. I'll just wait!' she whispered to herself.

Two guys were sitting in a truck nearby. "That old man Jakes was up to his old tricks again, picking up young girls, I see. He didn't get away with it this time." They laughed and moved on, not knowing that Geryl had heard everything that they had said or maybe they had wanted her to hear them.

She walked into the electric company office at four fourteen. As soon as she got into the house, she called her mother and told her the whole story.

"Do you want me to call the police?" she asked.

"Yes! I don't know his name, but I heard some gentlemen call him old man Jakes.

He was driving a light blue station wagon with yellow covers on the front seat. And, if they want I will give them a description of him." Geryl was now calm and had regained her composure.

Just hearing her mother's voice had given her a sense of security, protection, and love.

"He should be reported… whether they do anything or not." Geryl added. "Yes! Call the police!"

They never heard anymore from anyone.

THOUGHT: Beware of the grinning, bearing gifts – or rides.

THOUGHTS TO PONDER!

Dear Brittany,

This story is true. Try to remember that patience is a virtue and a Gift of the Holy Spirit.

Never accept a ride from any stranger. That was a lesson I re-learned. God took care of me that time. For me, he has always been there in times of trouble. Never fear, when trials come your way God will protect and keep you in His care. Stay close to God and abide in the love of the Almighty Savior Our Lord Jesus Christ. Read the Bible and pray every day. That Great God Almighty who parted the Red Sea and who raised Lazarus from the dead; will be with you all the time and every way. God is your refuge and your strength. You can't live without knowing God!

Lovingly,

Gram

XXXXXX

I'm a woman alone
But,
I don't want your bones!
Baby sitters fee,
Good luck charms,
Mon — ey!!!
Up . . . your . . . .nose
Bud . . . DY!!!

I job -
From eight to four
My own self . . .
And, am good at it, too.
Can "foot" my jive
And sacrifice
The "sugar t" I'd get from you.

Don't insult my femininity
With your offers of easing my pain.
To crap with your prick
Your jive time tricks
And the days you can sneak out is hard . . .
You and me, Babe, we ain't in the cards.

Spend your fancy dimes
And your pretty rhymes
With her who sits and waits
As for . . . running with me
Ha! I'm by choice fancy and free
Why, next week, I got me two dates.

If it's a slab on the side
That will fancy your pride
They stands on the street
And they waits.
It's a part of their humble discretion
And, shucks, man, it's their chosen profession.
Not mine...
And besides
Other women's men I don't want
Other women's problems I don't need.
The next effort you try... your cheap, jive time lines
Here's a lesson you need to heed:

A woman alone has pride of her own
And your respect, not your lying.
And, just don't believe cause she's
A woman alone
She need your unjust reward.
And is looking for something that's hard.

She's got it
Hard times
Hard roads to travel
Hard and heavy burdens to bear —
Your proposition smells "cheap" ...
Ready to sleep,
Bud — dy, how do you dare!

Through getting it all of off my breast
Perhaps through it all he meant no harm,
He figured it all masculine charm, and virility form.
Brother, I don't fancy being
Classed as a "pant — sy" and don't you
Forget it -
You worm!

THE LETTER

After Mother and Faye Jean moved to Connecticut, we spent our time between Seaport Town and North Haven. We wanted to spend all of our time in Seaport Town. Mom Minnie was there. And, everyone loved her. She was a short, heavy-set, round pleasant lady with a beautiful smile and effervescent personality.

She and I would sit around the kitchen table for hours talking like two old ladies. We simply adored one another and being together… in one another's company. The family would say, "Oh, there they go, again. They will sit in there and talk and talk and talk. What **do they** talk about?"

"Mom, how many children did your mother have?" Geryl asked.

"Honey, I don't know. She had so many I stopped counting." Mom Minnie smiled and added, "I am the oldest. Seriously, I do believe that she was pregnant at least to a twenty-one children. To look at her you would not have thought. She was tall robust and thickly built lady."

We talked about the family. When Mom Minnie was a little girl, the family moved from Crispus, Maryland to Seaport Town, Delaware. Her grandmother had been a slave who remained on the plantation after being granted her freedom by her slave master, Mr. Chomas Rose."

"Chomas?" Geryl inquired.

"That is what my Grandmother told me." Mom Minnie volunteered. "My grandmother was
Annie Rose and my mother Mary Annie Rose."

"You knew your grandmother, Annie?" Geryl exclaimed. "How exciting!"

"Grandma Annie, Mom Mary and I lived on the Rose farm until we moved to Seaport. We worked for Ms. Edith. Most days we did the cooking and cleaning; as well as the washing and ironing."

"You worked also?" Geryl questioned.

"I was only eight, but I had to help out. I can remember that Grandma Annie gave me a box to stand on so that I could reach the ironing board. I worked five days a week for one dollar and fifty cents. And, that was a lot of money." Mom Minnie told the story.

And this was how we talked most of the time… just about things.

"Geryl, will you please read this letter. It came in the mail yesterday." Mom Minnie slowly made her request.

Geryl read the letter, quietly. She then explained to her grandmother the contents of the letter. "Mom, this letter is a plea for you to write a letter in defense of Mr. Joseph Simmons who killed Uncle Norman. If he can get a positive response from you, the Parole Board will suspend his sentence and release him from prison, effective immediately. He may go to a half-way house for a couple of days or so."

"Um, I see." Mom Minnie pondered.

"What do you want to do, Mom?" Geryl could not imagine having to make such a difficult decision.

"Well, we'll write the letter. We can ask the people, board or prison officials to give him another chance. We have forgiven him." Mom Minnie had decided.

We sat and wrote, scratched and re-wrote. Finally, there at the kitchen table, we finished the letter that I read to Mom Minnie who said, "It sounds good to me. Let's mail it.

Freedom

I've been a slave all my life now —
Yet — I'm free!

I've been a slave all my life now.
Did you hear me?

I've been a slave all my life now.
I can't be free!

Liberty, pursuit of happiness,
What does it mean?

Equality, justice, inalienable rights,
Is that for me?

Endowed by their Creator?
God please help . . . .
them!

The persecutor, the racist, the bigot,
The suppressor, the white ones . . .
Please set them free!

Or else — I'll die
A slave . . .
In my grave? Yes. Me.

I've been a slave all my life now.
And, yet I'm free.

Gawjjones
1994

Bless Your Heart

We did not like North Haven or Connecticut – at all, period! We would have been content to spend the rest of our days in Seaport Town.

Well, to make matters worse, Mother had found some jerk to be her friend and companion... Yuk! Fran and I had not met him. Faye Jean did not l like him. She talked to us a little about him.

We just thought that mother would return to Seaport Town now that Gran Pop Will had died. We were wrong.

Mother came into the kitchen, whispering, "Geryl, did you and the girls eat the pork chops in the refrigerator?"

I could not understand the whispering and secrecy, "Yes!" was the plain and simple fact.

"Why? What's wrong?"

I could tell that mother was upset. She was blinking her eyes and looking – not in my directions.

"Patterson, said that he went to get his pork chops out of the refrigerator and they were gone." Mother continued to whisper.

"And?" was my one statement. "Who is Patterson? Is he your friend.?"

"Geryl, he will hear you." Mother was so nervous.

"I don't care!" with an indignant tone. "What kind of man visits with a woman knowing that she has children and then questions the children eating the food in the refrigerator. He does that?"

"Geryl..." mother tried to speak.

"Oh, no, Mother!" I was disturbed, greatly. "A decent man would try to help his woman with her children! What kind of man do you have here! You don't need him. If he can't help you, why are you letting him hurt you?"

"Now, Geryl, please."

"Wait a minute, Mother. Just tell him to wait." I turned to look at Fran & Faye Jean.

Mother was puzzled. She was blinking her eyes and avoiding our stares.

"Fran & Faye go in the bathroom. And, when they come out, you tell Mr. Patterson that he can have his pork chops back. We will even wrap them up for him in some fluffy paper."

We heard the front door slam. We prayed that our "intruder" had left permanently.

Mr. Patterson returned with two bags of groceries. Grinning and showing a mouth full of gold, he placed the bags on the kitchen table.

I'm glad that I did not thank Patterson for those groceries. That night he slipped into my room. Breathing heavily, he stood over me; about to pounce..

I lifted myself up straight in the bed. "What do you want, man? Why are you in my room? Did I invite you in here? What is wrong with you?"

"Your mother tells me that you are a virgin. I don't believe her." The Cad whispered.

"Speak up! Do you have something to hide?" I looked hard and strong into his eyes.

He tried not to look at me. I can smell a coward from a short distance.

"Let me tell you this, Mr. Patterson, for the one and only time. I won't ever repeat it, believe me. If you ever step foot in my room again, they will call you Mr. Short... not because of your height; but because of your short pants in your pocket. Do you understand me? Did I make myself clear?"

He stood there not believing what he had heard.

"Now, get out! GET OUT!" I screamed and then fell back to sleep.

When I got to Seaport Town, I told this story to my grandmother Mom Minnie who said to me, "Bless your heart, child! Bless your heart!"

THINKING

On most days, Gran Pop Waldin could not remember his name. Few folk knew the disease as Alzheimer's or dementia. But, Gran Pop suffered with both. He would watch television and laughed at all the people – no matter what. Pop could find something wrong with any one on the screen.

"Look," he would say. "That fool's got big lips!" And then he would laugh for a minute or more. He would then try to engage others in his conversation with the television.

Faye and I tried to reason with Pop. He did not hear or listen. He lived in his own existence and world.

It was Faye's sixth birthday. We celebrated with a family birthday party. Mother invited four children who lived in the first floor apartment. The children were dancing, singing and playing games. Pop, yelled out, "There is too much noise in here. I can't hear my brain talk and think. You children are keeping my brain from thinking."

We could not contain ourselves. That was so hilarious.

Several weeks later, we took Pop's body back to Seaport Town. The funeral was at Wesley Memorial. Most of East Seaport had forgotten Pop; but out of respect for the family, the towns folks visited, brought food, sent flowers, paying homage to our grandfather.

And just three week later, they did it again. Mother's oldest brother died. Uncle Raymond and Aunt Jeanette lived in New Jersey. Uncle Raymond spoiled my grandmother, his wife and his family. During the summer months, we spent time on the farm with Uncle Raymond.

He and Aunt Jeanette owned more than fifty acres of land near Pennsville. It was prime land that was in close proximity to the new highways and roads planned for that area.

Family, friends and members of the Jesus Is Lord Holy Spirit Church traveled to Seaport for Uncle Raymond's funeral. Our own Rev. James officiated and the pastor from Jesus Is Lord delivered the eulogy.

That Pentecostal church brought their musicians, choir, drummers, guitarist, and instruments. The church was jumping! "It sounded like a juke joint." some of the towns people said.

As soon as the preacher started the sermon, one of the ladies told her friend, "Hold my purse." She jumped up and shouted for about five minutes. Folks thought that mother was crying for her brother, but mother had laughed until the tears rolled down her cheeks.

Mother had heard the lady ask someone to hold her purse. Not too long after that, one of that lady's falsies fell on the floor.

Pop and Uncle Raymond were laid to rest at Greater Hope A.M.E. Church Cemetery. "The family plot looks like a small city out there," Alonza told Mom Minnie. "You people need to stop all that dying."

"Don't pay that fool no mind, Sister Minnie," Aunt Anna spoke quickly. "If he had good sense, he would be dangerous!"

We never heard from Aunt Jeanette ever again. She did not call or write or say anything. We never knew where to find her. She no longer lived on the farm. It was deserted. A "SOLD" sign was posted on the property.

"Now, there is no doubt as to what she did is there?" it was the resounding authoritative voice of Alonza. "She took the money and ran!"

XXXXX

Is life so grim
So pale
So sore
So dry
So pug
So quick
So slow
So strange
So retched
So cursed
So meek.
No!
Death's so
Absolute!

THE TRAIN RIDE

We were so happy, leaving North Haven to go home to Seaport. As we sat on that train, we prayed and dreamed that one day, Mother and Faye Jean would come back home to Seaport to live. We dreamed as hard as we prayed.

School would start in two weeks. With those thoughts in mind, we settled back on the train ride to hope, to pray and to dream. We imagined all the fun things that we would do at school and the many friends that we would see. We were more than excited. It was a great day to think, to ponder and - to dream.

The Last Stop

Shopping bag close to her knee,
Slept the old cleaning lady,
Tied from a hard day's work,
Her old black coat — grey faded.
O'er ten years,
Tis been the same
Up at dawn,
Half an hour each way.
Making n'er enough
To last from day to day.
This she dismissed
O'er pride and self esteem.
Pay the hour and fare got she
And the ride on the five fifteen.

Behind the Times,
With good intent,
The stiff white collar worker.
Then comes his friend,
The reading ends,
A quick run to the smoker.
And, perhaps,
Time permit
He added every time,
First on me,
Not today
I'll have a little lime.

The every other week riders,
Four in hats and furs.
O'er a game of bridge,
Shoes half off,
Noises from foundation popping.
To the best stores in town,
Then at Grays to dine.

Where tips cost more than a meal for two
At Kresky's Five and Dime.
The fattest one with the pretty face,
Rattling on about a diet.
The gaudy one in silk and lace,
Boasting of the price she'd pay to buy it.
The quiet one, with eyes so gay,
Nodding in firm accord.
The other one, it's hard to say
How she fit in the sward.

A regular besides myself
A retired conductor, he.
Knew all the bumps
The stops, the towns
Token in his hand
Began to make his rounds.
And e'er one ignored him
Supposing his senility.
He took the course
Each day the same,
The ride for him was free.

Two little boys excitedly twisting
Perhaps their first train ride,
To visit their grandma or uncle and aunt
Enjoying the countryside.
Began a game,
Counting the poles
Quickly shifting by:
One-hundred and three,
One hundred and four,
One-hundred and ninety five.
Soon grew bored
With the tiresome chore.
Falling asleep the ten year old
With open eyes, the older dreamed,
As the rode on the five fifteen.

In the dimly lit corner,
Pretense to be alone,
Two lovers, I imagine
Minds bent on their own.
Eyes gaily dancing,
Every word a kiss.
Arms tenderly enfolding
Moments filled with bliss.
Stealing a quiet week-end
Making each second compute.

A keen young man in uniform,
Home on his first leave.
The air and poise of boot camp,
His hands across his knees.
Not intently thinking,
But worried still and yet
Of what home would be like
How quickly we can forget.
Tugging relentlessly at his collar,
Choking, enhancing his speed.
Edging the nerve
To tip his hat
Or say a word,
To the girl who sat to read.

Obviously a co-ed,
Who'd threatened
Away from the scholastic drag -
She'd have a ball,
Enjoy her freedom,
Not one moment would lag.
The truth of the situation
There was n o more fun at home,
But, here she could hide her boredom
Her fate of being alone.
No sooner the two days over
Back among her friends
Invent a smashing invitation,
A grand and glorious week-end.

And the car door opened
Four new faces did appear,
The conductor tore each check
Out of habit he scratched his ear.
Comfort glistened in his eyes,
Sadness on his face.
This was his last ride,
And the five fifteen as well
Were soon to get that needed rest,
From years of toil and haste.
Last stop in ten minutes
Fort Junction straight ahead.
He yelled, grimaced,
Grabbed himself,
Fell to floor,
He's dead.

These were the only riders
In car thirteen on the train
As it pulled to make its last stop
In the blurry, chilly rain.

THE END

EPILOGUE

Dear Brittany,

FRIENDS

What is a friend?
Someone who doesn't pretend,
Who is strong within?
Who is there from beginning 'til the end?
When times get hard –
A friend is always on the ball…
Thru it all.
There are good friends,
And there are bad friends.
Trust in yourself –
So you and your good friends won't have to pretend…
And friendships will last until the end.
(Written by Brittany 2002)

Brittany enjoyed writing poems… her gift to all of us and God's gift to her. This poem was included in "From Our Hearts to Yours." And, we included it in our tribute to you. That homage read:

"Family was important to Brittany. She was rooted and grounded with strong family ties and relationships. Her mother was her best friend. Britt and Grandma Fran shared a love for elegance, fashion, glamour, dignity, and sophistication. Both Brittany and her Gram G. loved music and singing. We can still hear them as they, together, via the telephone, sang, "Order My Steps.'"

'Brittany's most fervent prayer was that her children would grow up in the church, know the love of God, and have a personal relationship with Jesus Christ Our Lord… just as she had experienced in her lifetime."

"During the three years that Brittany battled aplastic anemia and leukemia, she was strong and full of hope. She fought a good fight! When her body was aching and filled with pain, she got stronger."

We will continue to love you, Brittany. Oh how we will cherish those memories and moments together. Love never dies. Death cannot capture love. Our hands will continue to write… with thoughts of you as our mentor and our guide; however, remembering that our gifts and talents only come from the Almighty Omnipotent God.

Love,

Gram

Brittany
May 27, 1986 – September 25, 2012